BILL MOORE. '94

Contents

Foreword and Acknowledgements

In the course of my profession I have had the opportunity of salvaging odds and ends taken out of old houses, which would otherwise have been destroyed, and it was in this way that I began to accumulate obsolete and unwanted kitchen fittings and equipment, which originally formed the nucleus of my present collection.

I am fortunate to live in an 18th C. town house, where the dry cellars two floors below street level provide ideal space for display against white washed stone walls (see pages 84 and inside back cover).

I became particularly interested in and intrigued by the changes which occurred in the long established medieval traditions of cooking in, over, and in front of open wood burning fires — the downhearth, due to differing requirements for the smaller and more efficient coal burning bar grates, which were being introduced from the 17th C. onwards.

Bar grates were in turn to be superseded by the cast iron kitchen ranges which were being almost universally installed from the mid 19th C. prior to the present day gas, and electric stoves, and solid fuel, or oil cookers.

A detailed study of the changes from downhearth to bar grate has not as far as I am aware been made before.

I confess to being a mere amateur in this field, and apart from my own observations and experience, much of my knowledge on the subject has been augmented by visits to museums and discussions with antique dealers, both of whom have been extremely helpful and generous with their time and assistance.

I must also acknowledge information from various publications and in particular those books listed in the Bibliography on page 81, which will provide readers with much more detailed information than it has been possible to provide in this publication.

Nevertheless I hope that the descriptions and illustrations will enable readers to recognise similar items, and assist in preventing the discarding and destruction of interesting, if obsolete, utensils and fitments; which has now caused them to have a scarcity value which would have flabbergasted their original owners.

Attributing dates to kitchen by-gones is extremely hazardous as identical patterns were made in many cases over a period of time, sometimes of one or two hundred years or longer still. Therefore, where dates have been given they should be regarded as a general indication only, which to the best of my knowledge I believe to be reasonably correct.

I wish to acknowledge the assistance I have received from so many generous friends, whereby I have been able to acquire my collection, and also the encouragement I have been given in undertaking the production of this book.

I must also thank Ruth Milner who has contributed in no small way in deciphering and typing out my early and final manuscripts.

I am also particularly grateful to Aubrey Mills for his patience and skill in taking the photographs for the illustrations, which with a very few exceptions, which are noted below, are all taken from my collection.

I have also to thank those who have given permission for the reproduction of the following illustrations:

3.   'Dawn & Sunset' showing the cottage mantelpiece — The Royal Photographic Society, Bath.

13. 18th C. Bar grate — Co-existence, Argyle Street, Bath.

15. A model representation of a downhearth with its furnishings and fittings — Mr. E. Turner, Metalwork Department, Victoria and Albert Museum.

20. A 17th C. Chimney Crane — A. G. Fyshe Esq. of Sollershope.

66. A Yetling — Mr. Graham Nicholson, Curator, The Castle Museum, York.

69. A Cloam Oven — Hon. Alderman W. F. Authers M.B.E., of the Tiverton Museum.

I am also indebted to Miss Ilid Anthony and Mr. Eurwyn Wiliam of the Welsh Folk Museum for much of the information concerning Cloam Ovens, to Mr. Ross Noble of the Highland Folk Museum concerning the use of the Hanging Brander and to Mr. Roger Cobb for allowing me to include the 17th C. recipe for Bath Buns.

And finally my thanks are due to the Wiltshire Folk Life Society without whose inspiration and encouragement this book would not have been written, and without whose assistance publication would not have been achieved. For this reason any surplus proceeds which may arise will be devoted to their work on the restoration of the Great Barn at Avebury.

List of Illustrations

43. Iron pot stand 18th C.
44. Cresset topped andirons, baking pot and spit.
45. A black cast iron baking pot or spider.
46. A black cast iron cooking pot, with handle and spur to hang a spoon.
47. Types of pot handles.
48. Black cast iron kettle and kettle tilter.
49. 19th C. cast iron pressure cooker or digester.
50. Hot water cisterns in copper and cast iron.
51. Two copper kettles, a half kettle, and a water jug.
52. A Wasborough bell metal skillet size 4. 18th C.
53. Tin lined copper saucepans, a size 1 skillet, and two brass saucepans.
54. A glaze kettle. *c.* 1800.
55. A long handled iron downhearth frying pan, two tin lined copper frying pans, a serving pan and an iron frying pan.
56. Three hanging frying pans.
57. A steamer, mid 19th C.
58. A wire gridiron, shoe and asses ear mullers, waffle and wafer irons.
59. Griddle or girdle plates.
60. Gridirons, downhearth salamander late 17th C., and a coffee bean roaster for use with a down hearth.
61. A hanging brander.
62. Revolving trivet, or downhearth brander.
63. Types of bread oven doors.
64. A side oven *c.* 1780.
65. An elm dough trough.
66. A yetling.
67. A bread shelf or harnen.
68. An ash bent wood flour barrel, a horsehair sieve and an early hand cut elm scoop.
69. A cloam oven.
70. Iron and wood peels, and a dough paddle.
71. Bent ash standard dry measures.
72. Bread scales.
73. A thible, and two ridge rollers.
74. Tinder box.
75. Sundry metal implements.
76. Tinware.
77. Metal implements.
78. Sundry wooden implements.
79. Ditto.
80. Implements in horn and bone.
81. Cider drinking.
82. Cottage spoon rack.
83. Whetstone.
84. Steel meat skewers in original wall frame 18th C.
85. Wooden mousetrap.
86. Ditto.
87. Earthenware pots.
88. Miscellaneous kitchen accessories.

Historical Background

Until the middle of the 15th C. it was customary for the fireplace to occupy a free-standing position, both in the great halls, as well as in the dwellings of the peasants. This arrangement allowed more people to sit or sleep around the fire. Besides providing heat, the fire also had to serve for cooking, either on spits suspended in front or over the fire, or in pots hung from a rough tripod or some such similar device above it.

Smoke from the fire was left to find its own way out, although in larger halls louvres might have been provided in the roof. One of the reasons why early stools were kept relatively low, was that thereby one had a chance of sitting below the level of the smoke.

After 1450 it became usual for fireplaces to be built with chimneys contained within the thickness of the stone built gable walls. Sometimes an independent bread oven would be incorporated at one side. In districts where timber framed structures were used, a separate stone chimney was built with the fireplace at its base, abutting onto the wooden frame work; in larger houses the frame would be built round and supported on the central chimney stack.

As wood fires burnt more readily with a draught from below, fire dogs were used to raise the logs, and at the same time to prevent them from falling forward into the room. By 1500 this arrangement had become the universally accepted pattern for domestic buildings, and it was to continue with only minor modifications for the next two hundred years, and longer still in the countryside where wood remained readily available, and coal difficult to come by.

As will be seen later, many ingenious methods were developed to overcome the restrictions of having to cook on an open fire at hearth level, commonly referred to as downhearth cooking. Indeed, a great variety of roasted, fried, baked, boiled and grilled dishes were produced. Grilling was originally known as broiling, as it still is in the United States of America.

A special feature of downhearth cookery was that a proportion of it actually took place in the fire itself. The utensils used for this purpose were to become obsolete where coal burning bar grates were introduced in the 17th C. and particularly in the early part of the 18th C.

In towns firewood had become difficult to obtain and bar grates were being specifically designed for burning coal. For every ton of coal used in the 17th C., fourteen tons were produced in the 18th C., and in turn four times this amount was being mined in the early 19th C.; thus one can appreciate the rapid increase in the provision of, and the demand for, this type of fuel. In large cities such as London and Edinburgh coal was used as early as 1600 and in other towns coal was used for both heating and cooking from about 1700 onwards, although wood continued to be used in the country well into Victorian times, and for room heating until later still.

'Sea Cole' as it was referred to in London and elsewhere — owing to its having been carried by sea in the colliers, from Newcastle and the north — was becoming increasingly easy to obtain as a result of improved transport facilities; if, in some cases, the last part of the journey had to be made by waggons or even

packhorses. Coal was burnt in iron baskets (9) or cradles, it also had the advantage of being slower burning and more heat effective; but to burn satisfactorily it required a good upward draught. This was provided by the new type of bar grates, of a comparatively shallow depth from back to front.
In existing houses the larger and far wider wood burning cooking fires were replaced by the narrower bar grates which left room for the introduction of side hobs or even small independent side ovens (13). New houses were built incorporating fixed coal burning grates (11, 12), which were later to be replaced by Victorian cast iron kitchen ranges.
The earliest type of range is said to have been invented in 1780, and small side ovens had become quite common some fifty years before then. Nonetheless it was to take another seventy years before cast iron kitchen ranges came into general use, around 1850. The speed with which 'downhearth' cooking was to be superseded by what is sometimes termed 'up hearth' methods, with the consequent change in the age old cooking traditions, obviously varied considerably from place to place, and from one district to another, largely governed by the type of fuel, wood, peat, or coal which was most readily available.
However, the 18th C. Georgian developments in London, Bath and elsewhere all incorporated coal burning grates in their basement kitchens, as well as for heating the upper floor rooms.
Peat burns with a much lower heat intensity than coal or wood, but where it was obtainable locally, it could usually be freely cut by all. A method of cooking with peat was to develop, retaining some of the old features of the downhearth cookery, together with others peculiar to this type of fuel (66). In a few suitable localities it continues to be used up to the present day.
Before one considers in more detail the construction of these early types of cooking fires, and the equipment which was used with them, it is important to remember the drastic change in life-style brought about by the Industrial Revolution which had become established by the end of the 18th C. The social and economic structure of Britain underwent a major transformation from a self-sufficient agricultural community to that of an industrial nation with a rapidly increasing population dependent on imported food.
It should be appreciated that in the 18th C., the period with which we are mainly concerned, the number of people living in the British Isles was a great deal smaller than it is today. The national census first held in 1801, showed that Bath had a population of some 30,000, and was the ninth largest city in England. Bath was then in its heyday, and in spite of the great improvements in the turnpike roads, travelling still remained an expensive pastime. The journey from London to Bath of about 100 miles cost 90/- in a hired postchase, and 20/- on the public stagecoach. At this time the average farm labourer's wages amounted to no more than £40 a year, and those of servants from only an average of £5, although in addition they received their food and clothing, which was considerably more than their wages. In 1780 the wages of four servants, about the average for a town household, was £12.10.6 a year plus tax.
The head maid, an experienced servant £5.15.6. + 10/- tax.
The second maid, only received £2.10.0. + 10/- tax.
The man servant was paid £4.4.0. + £2.10.0. tax and finally a boy at 10/6.

In less than 200 years weekly wages were to increase by far more than those that were paid per year.

A small book entitled a 'Cooks Oracle' published in 1817 tabulated the annual expenses of a female servant as follows:

½ lb of tea per month and sugar per week	£3.10.0
4 pairs of shoes	10.0
2 pairs of black worsted stockings	4.0
2 pairs of white cotton stockings	5.0
2 gowns	1.10.0
6 aprons, 4 check, and 2 white	10.6
A bonnet, a shawl or cloak, pattens, ribbons, handkerchiefs, pins, needles, threads, thimbles, scissors, stays, stay tape, buttons and miscellaneous working tools, etc.	2. 0.0
A total for the year of	8. 9.6

It will be noted that tea and sugar accounted for more than a third of total expenditure.

In villages and rural communities people had of necessity to be largely self-reliant and self-supporting in order to survive.

Ordinary people had to face financial problems even more severe than those of today, and were constantly concerned with where their next meal was coming from.

From 1500 to 1800 wages had increased by four to five times, but wheat the basic necessity of life had increased by seven times. The cost of a quarter of wheat had risen from 43/- in 1792 to 126/- in 1812. Clothing and meat had risen by 15 times. Indeed, it has been claimed that but for the poor rate, from which assistance was given to no less than one fifth of whole population, rising in 1750 from one million pounds to two and a quarter million pounds at the end of the 19th century, we should have suffered a revolution comparable to that which took place in France.

The ingenuity of the common folk was astonishing and is reflected in their tools, often self made, and passed on from father to son, and so becoming all the more meaningful, forming as they did a vital and familiar part of their day to day existence.

To my mind their simple everyday utensils are for these reasons all the more interesting, if not poignant, providing an insight to our social history of not so long ago.

The Downhearth and the Bar Grate

Downhearth cooking fires required considerable space and on average, a cottage fireplace (1) would have an open hearth width of five to six feet, with a depth of around three feet, together with a clear height of about four feet six inches from the hearth level to the bottom of the wood or stone lintel.

In order that the fire could draw properly without undue smoking, a comparatively large flue of about three feet wide by two feet across was necessary. These flues which reduced in size towards the top were generally built straight so that the sky could be seen from below; a fact which helped the young boys who were employed to sweep the flues, but aggravated down draught.

Fireplaces in farms and larger houses were often bigger still, to allow two or three things to be cooked at the same time as well as maintaining a supply of hot water. They were therefore built to suit the occupier, only being limited by the available space. In some cases the whole gable end was used as a fireplace, with ingle nook seats on either side.

A common arrangement in a cottage which usually had an internal width of about fourteen feet, was for the fireplace to be slightly offset from the centre. This allowed for a bread oven to be incorporated at one side of the cooking hearth, and a winding spiral staircase on the other. A cross beam would often carry the first floor over, and would be built into the chimney breast over the fireplace lintel — a potential fire risk.

The staircase fitted into a space of about five feet and usually consisted of about eleven rather steep steps leading to the first floor, which was partly contained within the roof space. If more than one bedroom was required, it was customary for one to lead into the other. Dormer windows would be used (2), though if only one room was to be made this would be lit by a window in the opposite gable end to the fireplace, so avoiding the somewhat complicated dormer construction. Cottage windows were generally a good deal smaller than those used nowadays, in order to conserve heat.

At ground floor level a door shut off the bottom of the stairs, which otherwise led straight up to the room above. Although somewhat of a fire hazard, the risk was not so great, as the sill level of the bedroom windows was rarely more than ten feet above the ground, making escape relatively simple, provided one could squeeze through the window opening.

The staircase itself tended to follow the pattern of the old spiral staircases in castles, which had the newel on the right-hand side, with the bottom doorway on the left; these having been built to give the advantage to the defender at the top who was able to use his right arm to repel an intruder.

For practical purposes fireplace openings usually had a shelf above the lintel. This became known as a mantelshelf (3) from the habit of hanging a short curtain known as a mantle from it to assist in holding back the worst of the smoke which would billow down the chimney in a high wind. When complete surrounds came to be made with the shelf and sides together they were termed mantelpieces, a strange expression unless one knows its origin.

The downhearth cooking fire would usually be provided with some contrivance to prevent the back wall disintegrating due to the heat of the fire itself. Cast iron firebacks (4) were commonly used for this purpose as they also provided the additional advantage of reflecting the heat into the room.

Where cast iron firebacks were too costly, or unobtainable, as they were in remote areas, a hard flagstone was used to give a sloping back to the fire itself. This not only protected the back wall, but by using a really large slab the space behind could serve as a hot cupboard. Another advantage was that these flagstones could also be readily replaced from time to time without undue difficulty. Elsewhere a more permanent method might be adopted such as building the back wall with slates on their edges forming a herringbone or similar pattern which successfully withstood the heat.

The hearth would be furnished with a pair of iron firedogs known as brandirons (4, 6), which in effect controlled the width of the fire itself, and which as already mentioned held back the burning logs, as well as providing the necessary draught of air to allow them to burn satisfactorily. In every fireplace there would also be some form of fixture, if only a rod built in across the flue, so that pots and kettles could be suspended over the fire below.

Where spit roasting was required, an additional pair of dogs with hooks attached either at the back or the front, called spit dogs or andirons were placed on each side and in front of the fire to support the turning spit (4, 6). Trays had to be placed (16) on the floor below the roasts to catch the fat and dripping. Although spit roasting was claimed to be the best method of cooking meat as it sealed in the natural juices, it nonetheless tended to be a messy affair, which subsequent developments aimed to ameliorate.

In some instances andirons were finished with cresset shaped tops (5, 44) which are popularly supposed to have been used for heating drinks. Although they may have been used for this, it seems much more likely that their primary purpose was to hold receptacles containing the fat with which the meat had to be basted from time to time.

Towards the end of the 17th C. the fronts of the brandirons were sometimes joined with permanent bars (7), thus holding back the logs, which could be heaped up behind to provide a greater area of fire. An ingenious variation allowed the whole front of the fire consisting of two cross bars to be raised by the addition of one or two sets of additional bars, each hooking on to the one below (8) so that the front of the fire could be built up to the desired height to suit the type of cooking required. The basic two bar front was a favourite form for peat burning fires.

Although all these innovations improved the cooking potential, especially for spit roasting, they were not well suited to the use of coal, and the fire basket suspended between brandirons was the first step to cater for coal. This was soon replaced by baskets or cradles as they were sometimes called with their own feet (9) which made brandirons redundant, although andirons were still required to support the spits. Indeed coal burning fire baskets were used in the larger cities from 1600 onwards.

In the early 18th C. these fire baskets were abandoned in favour of fixed bar grates, built into the walls of the fireplace, and especially designed for the purpose of burning coal to the best advantage.

Bar grates (10) were usually made with the top bar capable of being dropped down through 90° to provide a two-bar shelf, on which to place pots and kettles.

This arrangement became known as the fall bar, and was to persist even after the introduction of cast iron kitchen ranges. These new bar grates were comparatively shallow from back to front, which enabled the depth of the fireplace openings to be reduced, and also the size of the chimney flues.

To economise on coal, the grates were provided with side cheeks (11, 12) which could be wound in or out by means of key operated ratchets, thus regulating the effective width of the fire and reducing it to a minimum when little or no cooking was required. In addition the grates were provided with retractable hooked bars at either end, which could accommodate spits (12) in place of the old andirons. It was these types of grate which were used in 18th C. houses, especially in the towns. In their final form towards the end of the 18th C., the side cheeks of the fireplaces also contained hobs (13) which could be wound inwards if required, providing useful platforms as well as giving a much neater appearance.

Whilst small cottages still only had one fireplace, houses were becoming larger, and additional fireplaces were introduced which were used for heating purposes only. For those additional fireplaces which still burnt wood, more ornamental and elaborate types of fire dogs with brass enrichments were used.

For fireplaces where coal was used in dining and drawing rooms, the built-in or free-standing fire baskets with brass fronts and legs were favoured. It was here rather than in the kitchen that the ornamental types of brass trivets, footmen and kettle stands were to be found.

It is interesting to observe that when coal burning basket grates became fashionable, the typical Georgian brass fronted fire basket (14) continued to reflect in its design the old arrangement of the pair of brandirons with the andirons projecting in front.

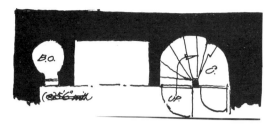

1. Downhearth Cooking Fires.

Slaughterford. Stone with wood lintel. 5' 6" × 3' 0".

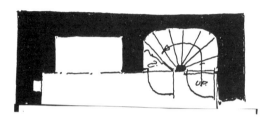

Biddestone. Stone sides and lintel. 5' 0" × 2' 9". Stairs now removed. Recess for tinder box on left.

Monkton Farleigh. Stone sides and lintel. 6' 9" × 2' 6". Original fireplace opened up and restored in 1979.

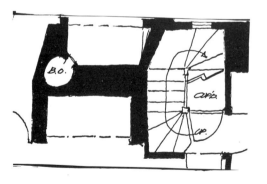

Chitterne. Stone sides with wood lintel. 6' 0" × 3' 0". A very old house. The staircase appears to have been added in the early 17th C. replacing a smaller one similar to the examples above. The second fire behind was also a later addition.

PLANS OF WILTSHIRE COOKING FIRES

2. Rock Cottage, Slaughterford, a modernised
16th C. cottage, with mullioned gable windows,
and bedrooms partly in the roof space.

3. Dawn and Sunset, a photograph by Henry
Peach Robinson *c.* 1865 showing mantel shelf.
Copyright The Royal Photographic Society.

4. Representation of a downhearth, the faggot supported on 18th C. brandirons, with matching andirons on either side. Ornamental cast iron fireback, much worn, probably late 17th C., a Renaissance pattern portraying Abraham about to sacrifice Isaac, and being prevented from so doing by the angel of the Lord.

In front is a 17th C. cast iron grisset, used for melting fat to make rush lights. Faggots of hazel or ash were popular from medieval times when a quick burning fire was required. At Stockton, Wilts., there exists a special wooden frame for compressing the sticks together, before binding.

14

5. An 18th C. spit engine, operated by a 14 lb. stone weight, the pulley cords being geared to rotate the spit wheel very slowly, the spit itself being supported by a pair of andirons.

Photo by Melanie Wilmot

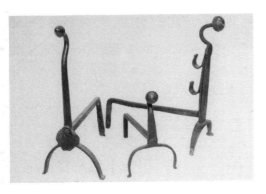

6. One of pairs of 18th C. brandirons, and of a pair of andirons.

7. A large pair of early 18th C. brandirons connected by four bars to enable the fire to be built up behind to improve cooking facilities.

8. An early 18th C. ingenious example of linked brandirons with three horizontal bars, but with two additional extensions to serve the same purpose as the previous illustration. A fire bar extension of a later date is shown supporting a brass lined pan.

16

9. An 18th C. fire basket, with a pair of spit irons. In the early 17th C. This was known as 'A cradell of iron for the chimney to burne seacole with'.

10. A simple bar grate from a farmhouse near Monmouth probably early 19th C. The top fall bar is easily distinguishable. Above is a cast iron hot water cistern with a brass spout and tap, hung from a small chimney crane, typical of those used with early bar grates. Below the fire bar extension is a brass ash shield or 'Tidy Betty'.

17

11. A built in adjustable bar grate from a house in Bristol, a typical example of the coal burning cooking fires used in 18th C. town houses, where coal was readily available. The shallow depth is apparent from the wedge shaped cheeks which were operated by pinions at the sides. Unfortunately the ratchets are missing as are the retractable spit arms, which would have fitted into the two holes on either side. The fall bar is in the down position.

12. A similar type to the previous illustration from Kington St Michael, Wiltshire, but the ratchets and spit arms are intact, and the side cheeks have removable hobs. These cheeks enable a little fire to be kept in, when a small amount of cooking only was required. In the front is a long pot rack or stand, the forerunner of later fenders.

13. A late 18th C. Adam style bar grate with retractable side cheeks and hobs, which in this case slid back into the cast iron side frames. The ultimate development of the type of grates shown in illustrations 11, 12. This grate is still in its original position in Argyle Street, Bath, a second fireplace also exists, which probably catered for spit cooking.

14. A brass faced 18th C. fire basket although used in a reception room, the pairs of urns are reminiscent of the tops of earlier brand and andirons, see illustrations 4, 9.

The furnishings of Downhearth Cooking Fires and their adaptation for use with Bar Grates

Before considering those items which were used purely for cooking purposes, mention must be made of those required to maintain the fire itself.

Curfews consisted of a semi-circular metal hood with a front lifting handle, which had been used from mediaeval times (a corruption of the French couvre-feu). They served a two-fold purpose, firstly as their name implies to cover up the fire at bed time to secure it against falling out or discharging sparks and so setting the house on fire, and equally important to keep the embers warm so that the fire could be readily rekindled the next morning. The problem of keeping the home fire burning during the day and smouldering only during the night was a very real one, as lighting it up again necessitated the somewhat tedious use of the *Tinder Box* (74). Rekindling the fire required the use of some form of artificial draught, which was provided either by a blowing tube or more usually by hand *Bellows* (17). Centrifugal blowers operated by a hand wheel were used for peat fires. Slow burning peat had a particular advantage as it smouldered for a long time, and some peat fires are said to have never gone out from one generation to another.

Wood forks with two prongs (17) and sometimes with a third prong at right angles to them to steady the logs, as well as *Tongs,* and iron shovels were used with downhearths. With raised bar grates a brass shield or fire guard sometimes stood below the grate to hold back and hide the ashes, and became known as a *Tidy Betty* (10). By the mid 18th C. sets of *Fire Irons* much as we know them today were being manufactured.

Cooking equipment as opposed to cooking utensils can be divided into three categories:

(a)   Those items which were used for cooking in the fire itself.

(b)   Those which were used to suspend containers of one sort or another above the fire.

(c)   The largest group of all, those which facilitated cooking in front of the fire.

(a)   *Baking Irons* (19) were short, three legged iron trivets for placing in the fire, to support baking pots and similar utensils which did not have legs of their own. They allowed the pots to be raised a short way above the hearth level, so that they could benefit from the heat below them. Both the stands and the pots themselves might be covered with wood embers, or peat blocks, which would be banked around, and sometimes right over the pot lids. A fork or a pair of tongs would be used to place the baking iron into position, and to remove it later on. Some baking irons had handles which no doubt made them easier to manoeuvre, and in these types the third leg was placed beneath the handle itself.

Brandreths (19) were also three legged iron trivets, having flat round or triangular tops, on which pots and pans, and more especially griddle plates could be supported over the top of the fire. Their longer legs distinguish them from baking irons. Brandreths are sometimes confused with standing trivets which were used for placing things on, at the side or in front of the fire to keep them warm. Brandreths are always very simply constructed, and can often be recognised by the fact that their feet have been worn away by the heat of the fire. Baking irons and brandreths could only be used in open wood fires, and so became obsolete when the downhearth was replaced by coal burning bar grates.

(b) *Pot Hangers* (18) of one sort or another were used for hanging pots, kettles, water cisterns etc. over the fire. The simplest forms were hooked rods, or chains suspended from an iron rod built into the chimney flue. A common method, especially in the North Country, was a chain of flattened wrought iron rings, with a hook at either end, sometimes known as *Jumping Rings*. They could be adjusted easily to whatever height might be required to carry the pot over the fire below. This method of suspension is said to date back to the Iron Age. Of all the other varieties, perhaps the best known is the saw toothed *Adjustable Ratchet,* or *Tramel,* which came into common use from 1600 onwards, which also provided a simple and easy method of adjustment.

Chimney Cranes provided an alternative to pot hangers, and were an improvement in so far as they allowed horizontal as well as vertical adjustment. They were known also as sways in Scotland and the North Country.

In its earliest and simplest form the crane consisted of a single horizontal arm (20) which could travel through 90°; but although simple it required a heavy iron bar, and an especially strong hinged fixing. It was therefore superseded by the bracket type, which could be made of lighter construction and could be much more easily and securely fixed to the back wall of the fireplace. The larger sort (21) were used over downhearths, and were often made with a decorative finish; they provided for a double adjustment either horizontally as well as vertically, and sometimes even in three directions, whereby the whole supporting bracket could be moved backwards and forwards on a wheeled track. These elaborate and no doubt costly cranes would have been used in the larger establishments where a substantial amount of cooking was undertaken. A special *Crane Hook* (15) was hung at the side of the fireplace, with which to manipulate and adjust the cranes which became hot from the heat of the fire below.

Bars were no longer built into the flues serving bar grates which were in any case smaller than those used for downhearths. But small chimney cranes were widely used, and were especially popular for supporting the black iron kettles and their accompanying tilter (10, 22).

Before leaving the subject of cranes, mention must be made of another small type of crane which was used from the late 18th C. onwards, and even with kitchen ranges, for suspending bottle jacks (see under Spit Engines) and known as *jack racks* (22). The commonest form of a jack rack was a small hinged bracket of iron or brass which was fixed onto the face of the fireplace lintel. Some Victorian ones in brass tended to become very fussy and ornate. Another type took the form of an iron clamp for screwing on to the mantelshelf, with a hook below which could slide backwards and forwards.

(c) *Spits.* The principal item in our third category, equipment for use in front of the fire, is undoubtedly the spit. The simplest took the form of a thin iron bar, one end having a sharp point which could pierce through the meat, and the middle part flattened out like a sword blade to prevent the joint from swivelling around. A two pronged fork which could be adjusted along the length of the spit was often added to serve the same purpose. Cranked handles were introduced for use by the turnspit or scullion, usually a young boy, whose duty it was to keep the spits turning on their supporting andirons, so that the meat was evenly roasted on all sides. This was obviously a very hot undertaking in front of the large fires, and in mediaeval times, a straw shield, similar to those used for archery practice, was soaked in water and mounted on a stand to protect the turnspits, and make their work more tolerable. Towards the end of the 17th C., spits were being fitted with a wooden wheel at one end instead of the cranked handle, which could take a pulley rope operated by one of the forms of spit engine. Those early wooden wheels being somewhat vulnerable, were later replaced by iron ones (44).

A further development took the form of the addition of a central iron cage or cradle fixed to the spit in such a way as to allow the joint to sit inside the cage (24). Forks held it steady, and the sides of the cage or basket screwed together, so that the meat was secure inside. Spit roasting in a horizontal position continued until ranges with their own built-in ovens came into common use and even then traditional spits were sometimes incorporated in larger establishments. A humbler type of apparatus should perhaps be mentioned, known as a *Dangle Spit* (25). It was a wirework contraption with a large hook at the bottom for hanging the meat, and four smaller hooks above to hold basting suet. It could be operated by a simple twisted cord, or by a bottle jack (see under spit engines). The earliest type of *Spit Engine* seems to have been the dog operated treadmill, a large wheel shaped cage operating a pulley rope, which in turn rotated the spit below in front of the fire. The treadmill was fixed well to the side of the fireplace, the cage being about three feet in diameter. Although at one time said to be very popular, few cages have in fact survived. One without its pulley can be seen at the George Inn, Lacock, Wiltshire. Such a contrivance had its obvious drawbacks, although it continued in use for some considerable time. An alternative weight operated type was introduced in the 18th C. These simple hand-made machines were usually operated by a stone weight of fourteen pounds (5); it may be coincidental that fourteen pounds became known as a stone. The engine was fixed to the wall and operated in a similar manner to a clock, the pulley rope being geared to allow the spit below to revolve very slowly. A more elaborate form of engine was used in some larger houses, known as a *Smoke Jack*. It was operated by a form of horizontal windmill built into the chimney flue; the vanes were set in motion by the hot air rising from the fire below, which in turn were geared to operate the pulley of the spit. Although ingenious they must have been expensive to instal, having to be built into the chimney; thus they remained something of a rarity. Another disadvantage was that they required a constant and considerable amount of rising hot air to operate, which could only be maintained by a very large fire, which would have required frequent replenishing.

With the advent of bar grates another type of simpler clockwork engine in a brass case was devised for roasting meat in a vertical instead of a horizontal position. This was known as a *Bottle Jack* (25) owing, presumably, to its similar shape and size. A key inserted into a hole in its side operated the mechanism. Bottle jacks had a hook on the top by which they were attached to the jack racks (see above). A cast iron wheel hung from the bottom fitted with a central hook, with four smaller basting hooks round the circumference. This wheel rotated first one way and then the other with an audible click as it changed direction; the absence of the clicking sound reminded the cook that it required rewinding, but this only occurred infrequently, as fully wound it would operate for a period of nearly two hours. The iron wheel could be detached so that the bottle jack could be used with a single hook, or with a dangle spit if preferred (28). Although sometimes fixed above downhearths, bottle jacks were more commonly used with bar grates. The final type of spit engine was a brass cased clockwork machine, mounted on the wall with a bar sticking out on one side, made around 1840 (25). The arm held one or more pulley wheels which operated the spits below, which in turn were held in position by retractable arms incorporated in the grate. Again the gear wheels were so adjusted as to allow the spits to revolve very slowly.

The great disadvantage of all forms of spit roasting was the necessity of having a drip tray below the rotating meat, which had to be well basted and would no doubt have spattered fat over a wider area than that covered by the tray (16). To overcome this *Reflector Ovens* (26) were introduced towards the end of the 18th C., which incorporated their own trays, containing built-in sumps from which the fat and gravy could be drained off. Moreover these portable tin ovens were shielded on all sides except for that which faced the fire.

The early low level types were used in front of a downhearth, but could also be used on a stand in front of bar grates; they had a built-in spit with a cranked handle which could be adjusted by means of a side pin pushed into a series of holes round a plate on one side, thus allowing the joint or bird to be rotated, but this periodical change had to be effected manually. To enable this to be done without having to disturb the oven, a hinged inspection door was provided in the back of the screen on the side away from the fire.

Smaller types commonly known as *Dutch Ovens* (27) were also made in tinware for cooking chops, small birds, etc. and these too could be stood on trivets or fire bar extensions in the case of bar grates. Some of these also had lift up backs to facilitate inspection.

A much larger portable oven was to evolve later, known as a *Hastener* (28) having its own legs, so that it could be placed right in front of the bar grate fire. It too had its back inspection door, and removable drip tray, but had the additional advantage of being able to accommodate a bottle jack, or other revolving devices such as the Victorian 'tubular roasting jack and crescent flyer.' As its name implies, the hastener was a speedier and economical type of oven, which could also be used in front of kitchen ranges, and was still being made at the beginning of the 20th C.

Grilling or *Toasting Forks* (30) standing in front of the fire were employed from early times. Primitive standing toasters consisted of two or three forks on a vertical support let into a domed shape block of wood, the forks being connected to a horizontal slide so that they could be pushed nearer the fire, or withdrawn as required. Later the same sort of arrangement was made entirely of iron, on a flat base, and the fork itself could also be moved vertically. There is considerable similarity between these toasting forks and rush nips, as the early form of rushlight stands were also let into blocks of wood. Yet another form was the downhearth toaster with a revolving head (29). Free standing, multiple toasting or grilling racks were developed with a large number of hooks (30) set in two or three rows, in some cases incorporating their own drip tray.

Bar Toasters (31, 32, 33) as their name implies were used with bar grates. They had clips to attach them to the front fire bars and had several rotating hooks, which enabled the object being cooked to be turned about, and could at the same time be manoeuvred to whatever distance from the fire was thought desirable. Some were known as lark spits, and are to be found in both iron and brass, and were particularly suitable for roasting smaller birds etc. But as with spits, they too had the disadvantage of requiring drip trays which would have been placed on trivets below.

An alternative type of lark spit was made towards the end of the 18th C., whereby the four hooks could be rotated mechanically by gear wheels. These were fixed to a separate shaft, which was turned by a brass knob.

Fire Bar Extensions The earliest type was known as a *Cran* (34) and consisted of an open work wrought iron platform which hooked on to the top fire bar, but unlike the later models, the platform was arranged to fit over the fire itself, instead of forming a front rack (10) on which to stand various utensils.

Plate Warmers (see also under trivets) took various forms, such as the stand with a reflecting brass sheet below, to throw the heat upwards onto the plates or dish which required to be kept warm (39). In the early 19th C. a boxed in type similar to a portable oven was produced which with its elegant lion mask handles was used in the dining room or parlour. It would also have been particularly useful for keeping muffins etc. warm (42).

Trivets. Apart from the cooking pot, the commonest item of kitchen equipment must surely have been one of the varieties of trivets. Their history is a long one, for instance a trivet from the grave of King Philip II of Macedonia although some 2,300 years old is almost indistinguishable from that used in the 18th C. in this country.

As its name implies the trivet was basically a three-legged stand or tripod, originally in iron. Its three legs like those of a milking stool allowed it to stand firm on any surface however uneven. A common 18th C. expression 'true as a trivet' was derived from this characteristic.

A trivet (35) was used to hold pots and other utensils in front of, and beside the open fire, and by mediaeval times it had acquired two other varieties, the baking iron, and the brandreth, both having circular or triangular tops, which have previously been mentioned.

In the 18th C. a 'super trivet' (37) called a *Cat* was used. It took the form of a double tripod with six legs, each leg screwing into a centre steel ball. It was so made that however placed it would always stand on three of the six legs, the upper three legs forming a cradle to accommodate plates etc. for keeping them warm. This ingenious device was presumably called a 'cat' due to the fact that it always landed on its feet however positioned.

Standing trivets offered considerable scope for ornamentation, especially as regards the tops where later examples with pierced plates replaced the simpler forms. The three legs were strengthened with intermediate ties and the front leg or legs became cabriole shaped and such examples are known as *Footmen*. Square and oblong tops although still referred to as trivets often had four legs and from this type larger sized pot stands were developed. Other forms became plate warmers or specially shaped kettle stands.

The more ornamental four-legged types made in brass and also called footmen as well as the brass folding types known as *Gypsies Trivets*, were designed for, and used in the dining rooms or parlours rather than for use in the kitchen (36).

Some ingenious person invented an open framed platform which was supported by means of a fixed semi circular top handle somewhat similar to those used for supporting cooking pots, and these became known as hanging trivets, in spite of the fact that they had no legs at all; in the West Country they were sometimes called a *Hanging Brandis* (23). For the so-called 'revolving trivet', (62) see under gridirons.

A variation of the trivet was the four-legged square or oblong topped *Pot Stand* (43), a utilitarian object usually made of flat iron bars, it provided a good deal more space than the conventional trivet. The long variety were eventually modified and turned into *Fenders* for bar grates.

With the advent of the raised coal burning bar grates, which became universally used in towns by the mid 18th C., the old fashioned type of standing trivet continued in favour, as they were useful for supporting small reflector ovens, and other items in front of the fire bars.

As time went by, however, some three legged trivets were made with hooks added to the back of the top platforms, which gave their owners the option of using them in the traditional way, or alternatively of hooking them directly on to fire bars.

Later still the hooks were fitted to a frame only which supported the trivet top or platform, allowing it to slide nearer to or further from the fire, as required. These contraptions were a logical outcome, but once more in spite of their lost legs, continued to be referred to as *Bar Trivets* (33).

Again the more ornamental types made in brass (38) were destined for parlours, to hold copper kettles, or half kettles, to provide a quick source of hot water to replenish the tea pots; wherever a coal grate with fire bars continued in use, these so called bar trivets remained in favour.

By 1850 when built in ranges came into common use with their side hobs and centre barred grate, the old three legged standing trivet was no longer to be found in the kitchens. Another form of trivet however with three short legs was to be revived, and to become universally popular, namely the brass flat iron, or kettle, stands; these like the irons were usually supplied in pairs. They too lent themselves to all sorts of ornamental pierced tops, often incorporating the popular heart motif.

At the Great Exhibition of 1851, a type of pressed steel four legged trivet was introduced which could be pressed out in a single operation; this novelty was to intrigue and astonish our Victorian forefathers, who would no doubt have been even more amazed at the elaborate car bodies and other pressed steel items which are commonplace today (40).

After this few trivets were made and were mainly in brass, as they were for ornamental rather than utilitarian use.

And so the long history of the trivet was to peter out, and those that still remained in households served only as decorative reminders of days gone by.

Right:

15. Model of an 18th C. downhearth cooking fire. Crown Copyright Victoria and Albert Museum.
Reading from left to right;

Forefront—
(1) Standing rushlight holder on wooden base.
(2) Downhearth toaster.
(3) Bread stand for browning off flat loaves.
(4) Skillet in cast bronze.
(5) Iron plate warmer with revolving frame.

Hanging at sides —
(6) Meat fork.
(7) Ember tongs for removing embers from the fire to obtain a light.
(8) Double hook for manipulating a hot chimney crane.
(9) Hearth tongs.

Inside opening on floor —
(10) Pipe kiln for purifying clay pipes.
(11) Pair of brandirons or firedogs to support logs.
(12) Pair of andirons or spit dogs for supporting a spit with adjustable pronged fork to hold the meat and with an early wooden pulley wheel connected by cords to the spit engine above.
(13) Cast iron fireback dated 1584.

Inside opening, hung from above —
(14) Kettle tilter on adjustable pot hanger to allow water to be poured from kettle without its removal.
(15) Adjustable saw-toothed type pot hanger or tramel with elaborate ornamentation.
(16) Cast bronze cauldron suspended by a chain from an ornate chimney crane.
(17) A simpler version of 15 above.

On or over mantelshelf —
(18) Spit with adjustable pronged fork and pulley wheel.
(19) Spare spit shaft.
(20) Table type rushlight holder combined with candlestick on wooden base.
(21) A spit engine or spit jack. Worked by a weight at the end of a cord wound round the drum, which is geared up through spur and worm gear to a governor. This enables the spit to turn very slowly at a uniform speed.
(22) Tinware tinder box (late 18th to early 19th C.) to hold steel flint and tinder, with a candlestick on the lid.

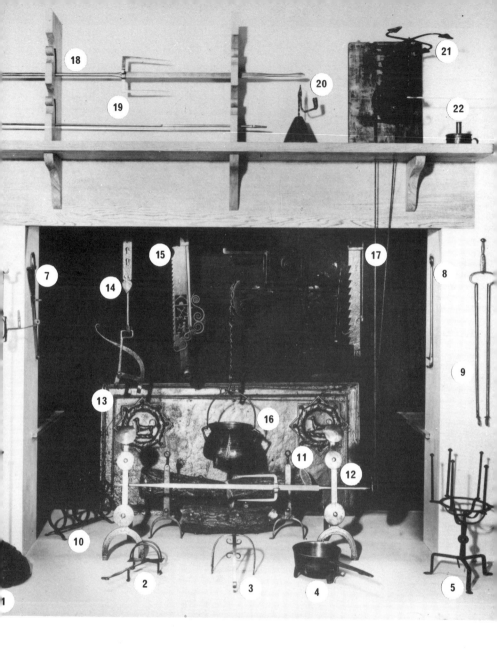

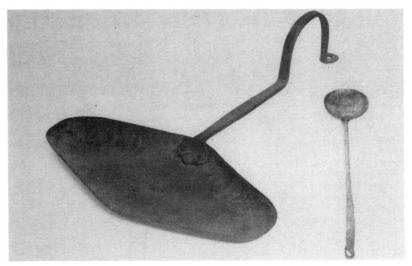

16. A small 18th C. drip tray, and typical basting spoon.

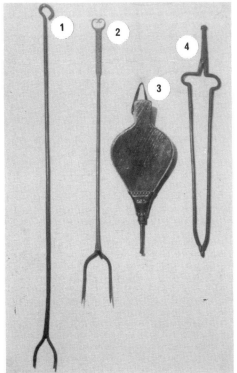

17. Tools for the wood burning downhearth. (1) An iron double pronged wood fork. 18th C.; (2) Similar with a projecting prong to steady the logs 18th C.; (3) A pair of bellows 19th C.; (4) A pair of tongs 18th C. Note. 'Fier sholves' and 'pairs of tongues' were used for 'seacole cradells' from the early 17th C.

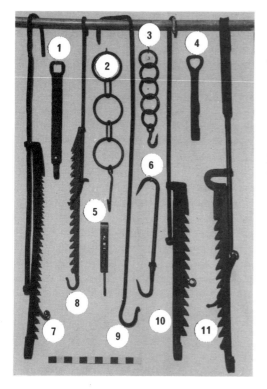

18. Pot Hangers. (1) Bar type with single hook for use with small crane; (2) Chain for hanging pot for use with out door cooking; (3) Jumping rings; (4) Double hook variation of item 1; (5) Adjustable ratchet hook for use with small crane; (6) Top and bottom hooks for similar use. The bottom hook swivels; (7) Ratchet hook or tramel with 24 teeth and curling end to ratchet; (8) Ditto with plain ratchet and 15 teeth; (9) Plain hooked end hanging rod; (10) As item 7 but with 14 teeth; (11) As item 8 but with 13 teeth.

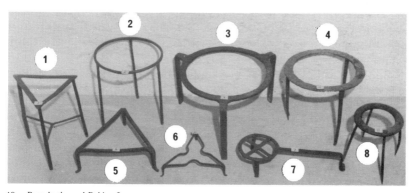

19. Brandreths and Baking Irons. (1) Triangular topped brandreth; (2, 3, 4, 8) Circular topped brandreths; (5, 6) Triangular topped baking irons; (7) Round topped ditto with handle.

20. Original cooking fireplace. Sollershope, Herefordshire. Early heavy single armed crane, with later double action crane supporting a pan on the right hand side, together with sundry other hearth furnishings.

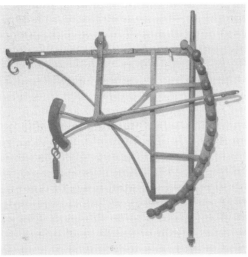

21. 17th C. three directional downhearth chimney crane. The small top wheel enables the crane to move forwards and backwards, the lever arm and studded crescent up and down, and the main supporting pivot through an angle of 90°.

30

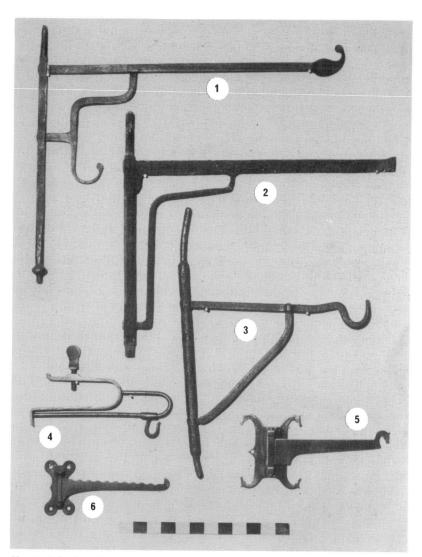

22. (1 – 3) Smaller chimney cranes or sways for use over bar grates especially for suspending black iron kettles on small pot hangers or tilters; (4) Jack Rack. Clamp type for fixing to mantelshelf; (5) Brass Jack Rack. The back plate decorated with the heads of four riding horses. The crane arm with the head of a cart horse; (6) Common black iron type of jack rack with saw toothed top to crane arm.

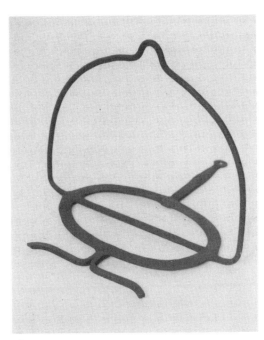

23. A hanging brandis. A trivet top with a handle which could be suspended from a hanger above the fire, instead of on three legs.

24. A basket or cradle spit, operated by the iron pulley wheel, supported on a pair of andirons or spit dogs. The basket is in the open position, the joint would be secured to prevent it from turning by the fork on the right. The top and bottom racks by loosening the end screws could be bent together to form a four sided cradle.

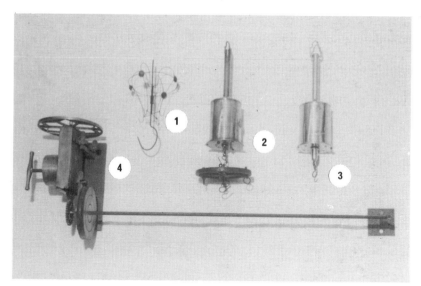

25. (1) 18th C. iron wire dangle spit, with cast lead enrichments, having four small hooks to take fat for basting above the main meat hook 10¼ " high × 5¼ " diam. Discovered under the floor boards of a house in Trim Street, Bath; (2) Brass cased clockwork spit or 'bottle jack' complete with original cast iron suspended ring with four small hooks on the outer ring, and one larger centre hook; (3) Similar to 2 above but without bottom ring (see also illustration 28); (4) Brass cased clockwork spit engine *c.* 1840. 'Patent Revolver Economic Roasting Spit' with rotating rod and one wooden pulley wheel.

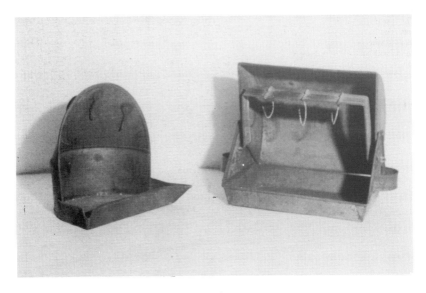

Top, left:

26. Low level early type of Reflector Oven, for use with down hearth fireplace. The front was placed up against the fire. The inspection door at the back is partly open. The sump in the bottom tray has a spout attached for draining off the liquids. *c.* 1775 or later. From Bideford, N. Devon.

Bottom, left:

27. Two examples of small tin reflector or Dutch ovens, if as is likely they were used in front of a bar grate, they would have been placed on standing trivets, or on a fire bar extension, or bar trivets. The top shield of the left hand examples tips forward, as does that of the one on the right, in this case the bar holding the three hooks is also adjustable. Both have handles on the back which do not show in photograph.

28. A Tin Hastener from Monkton Combe, nr. Bath, Height 4' 6" × 1' 9½" wide. Probably last half 19th C. Cost in 1850 — 21/9d. The rear inspection door is slightly ajar. The removable sump is clearly shown. A brass bottle jack is fitted on top with an early wire dangle spit.

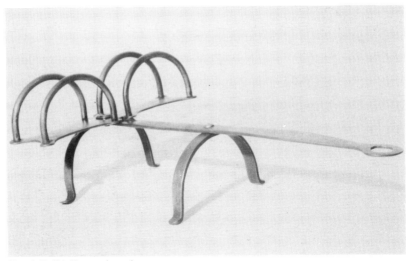

29. A 17-18th C. wrought steel
downhearth toaster with a revolving
head. 14″ long by 8″ across.

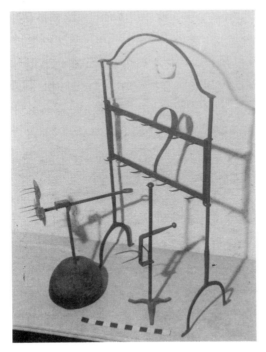

30. Two examples of standing
toasters, that on the left is the
earlier, the arm holding the three
hooks can be adjusted horizontally;
the base is a block of wood 7″ in
diameter. The overall height being
1′ 6″. The steel example is just over
1′ 6″ high with a single adjustable
double hook on a tripod base. In
this case the fork can be adjusted
vertically. The toasting rack with 7
hooks on each of the two bars,
almost certainly had an iron frame
below, to carry a drip tray, the
holes for which can just be seen
about half way between the top of
the hooped legs and the bottom
bar. 1′ 8″ × 2′ 11″ high. The two
bars have vertical adjustment.

Top, right:
31. 17th C. Hook on Bar Toaster
probably Scottish for baking
bannocks and small flat scones.
(Handle missing). Distance from
fire adjustable.

Bottom, right:
32. Late 18th C. Hook on Bar
Toaster also probably Scottish.
Angle and distance both adjustable.

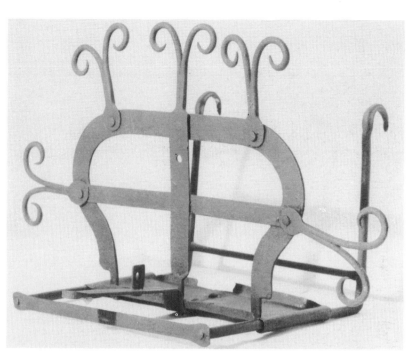

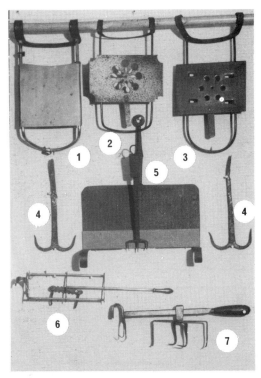

33. Fire Bar Trivets, Griller and Cellar hooks. (1) Brass Platform sliding on hooked frame; (2, 3) Pierced iron platforms on hooked frames; (4) Two late 17th C. cellar hooks; (5) Late 17th C. fixed iron platform with adjustable fork; (6) 18th C. brass 'lark spit' with swivelling hooks; (7) Early 18th C. iron griller with swivelling hooks and wooden handle.

34. Early 18th C. wrought iron fire bar extension or 'Cran' for fitting over rather than in front of the fire, for use with coal burning baskets or cradles.

35. A selection of 18th C. standing trivets. (1) Circular top 11″ diam. × 1′ 3½″ high.
(2). Rectangular top with ornamental front leg, this type was known as a footman. Top 11″ × 8½″ × 1′ 2″ high. (3) Early triangular top with shaped legs and intermediate support. (4) Simple round top with 3 cross bars and very splayed feet, 10″ diam. × 1′ 0″ high. (5) Shaped round top, legs having intermediate support, 1′ 0″ high, to hold a kettle.

36. A brass topped trivet, with a turned wooden handle, and iron frame and legs, also fitted with hooks so that it could be placed up against the fire bars of a bar grate. A pierced top has an anthemion design c. 1815. A folding all brass trivet, which allowed it to hang flat on the wall, when not in use, sometimes described as a gypsy's trivet.

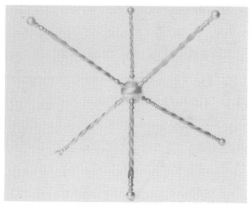

37. A steel cat c. 1750, each arm and aperture separately marked to ensure a correct fit, used as a plate stand or to hold a basin or saucepan, however placed it always stood on three feet, with the other three feet for supports.

38. An elaborate brass topped bar trivet, sliding on a brass frame, attached to a horse shoe shaped iron plate with hooks at either end *c.* 1800.

39. An iron framed plate warmer with brass reflector. Top 1' 0" × 7½", height 1' 6".

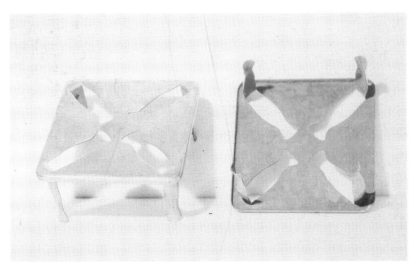

40. A pair of pressed steel trivets *c.* 1850. An early example of this type of industrial technology.

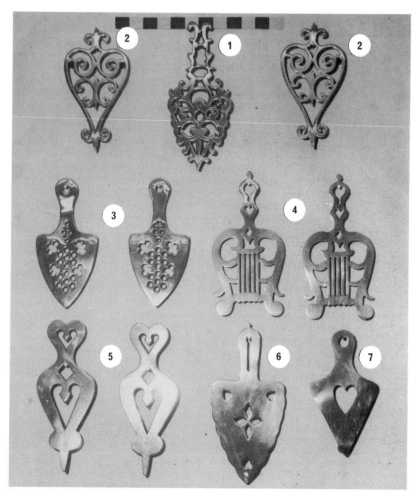

41. Iron or Kettle Stands Mid 19th C.
(1) Pierced over all pattern with long handle;
(2) A heart shaped pair with openwork pattern;
(3) A spade shaped pair with pattern of round
holes; (4) A lyre shaped pair; (5) A pair with
heart patterns on main body and handle; (6) A
single stand with pierced centre pattern and
three small hearts, handle cut to allow stand to
be hung up; (7) A single simple pattern, with
large pierced centre heart and round hole in
handle.

42. Late 18th C. or early 19th C. tole oven type plate warmer on cabriole legs. Brass lion headed carrying handles. Probably Pontypool manufacture, the open side stood against the fire bars.

43. 18th C. iron pot stand 22" long × 17" wide × 12" high. These stands were later superseded by low fenders, with top bars.

Cooking Utensils

In ancient times, when the threat of invaders necessitated a speedy retreat to secure strongholds or to the surrounding woodlands, with the likelihood of the rude dwelling being destroyed, the cooking pot, or crock as it was sometimes called, would be quickly buried with any valuables or money placed inside, in the hope that they could be retrieved later on, when the danger had passed. It was from such circumstances that the Irish legend originated of the mythical crock of gold to be found where the rainbow ends.

The *Cooking Pots* used in the 14th and 15th C. were usually made of bronze, or a bronze alloy such as bell metal. They had three fairly long legs to enable them to stand well up in the fire, and in addition they had side ears to accommodate a handle, usually in iron, to enable them to be suspended over the fire.

Later the commonly used types of cast iron pots had shorter legs (46). They were made in two halves over a clay core and the welded side seams are clearly visible. They also had a cast iron lid with its own handle, as well as the semi-circular iron handle to carry the pot itself.

The cooking pot can justly claim to be the one basic and indispensable utensil, and was used for heating water, as well as for all sorts of cooking purposes.

The average size of the cast iron pot was ten to twelve inches in diameter, and eight to ten inches in height, and was used with or without a lid. Much larger sizes however were used for special purposes.

In cottages, meat was usually pot-boiled rather than roasted; the accompanying vegetables were placed in small linen bags or nets suspended in the boiling water, either from rods laid across the top of the pot, or hooked on to the sides. Wrapped suet puddings, or dumplings could also be cooked at the same time, so that apart from bread, the whole meal could be produced from the single pot.

The liquid left over after the cooked food had been removed was known as pot liquor, and this together with bread and potatoes formed the major part of the diet of the children of poorer classes.

Snacks of bread and ale, sometimes with a little cheese, which has always been a comparatively expensive item, were the order of the day, with only occasional hot meals of bacon, rabbits, etc. Anything edible which the countryside could provide was eagerly sought after, and many things were eaten then which would not be contemplated nowadays.

In 1797 the weekly expenses of a farm labourer, his wife and children, were as follows:

7 ½ gallons of flour 2/3d plus yeast for making bread 4d	6/7
1 lb of bacon 8d which with greens, potatoes etc from the garden would last for 3 meals	8
Tea 1 oz. at 2d, and small beer at ½d per quart	2¾
¾ lb of sugar 6d, ½ lb butter or lard 4d	10
¼ lb soap at 9d per lb 2¼d, and ⅓ lb candles (tallow) 3d	5¼
Thread, materials for mending and miscellaneous	3

No cheese is mentioned.   9/2

His basic wage was 7/- per week, with some free milk, plus an average of 1/- per week overtime, work done by his wife and children had to make up the balance.

Baking Pots (44) were made in heavy cast iron, and were placed in the fire, which was banked up around and over the top. Where no bread oven existed they were used for baking bread, cakes and buns. Those with three legs were known as Spiders. (45).

The semicircular *Pot Handles* (47) which fitted into the side ears, were no doubt originally made to suit the individual pot; however in the 18th C. onwards adjustable handles were being made which could fit different sized pots. In larger households racks were fitted to hold a dozen or more handles which could be used for hanging a variety of utensils including pots, pans, digesters and cisterns.

All *Pot Handles* (47) share the common characteristic of hooks at the ends of the arms, which went through the two fixed ears of the pot, sometimes both hooks were bent in the same direction, whereas others were made in opposite directions, which provided a more secure fixing.

There are a number of variations which mark the development of pot handles:

(a) The plain bar handle with hooks at either end suitable for an individual pot size.

(b) A similar one but with an added ring at the top of the handle, which made it easier to hook onto a pot hanger.

(c) Both arms instead of being made in one piece were made separately and linked together at the top, giving some measure of flexibility. This type does not appear to have been very common.

(d) The common type of adjustable handle, in which both arms and the suspension hook are held together by a bolt at the top, which gave the maximum flexibility, enabling the handle to be fitted to a considerable number of pot sizes.

(e) A similar one to the above, with a spur added to one arm, on which a spoon could be hung, a comparatively rare type.
Metal kitchen spoons usually had holes in the top of the handles, so that they could be hung up.

Whilst this seems a logical sequence of developments, the different types may simply be local variations. The fourth type was undoubtedly the most widely used.

Before leaving the subject of pots, mention should be made of an early sort of pressure cooker, known as a *Digester* (49). It was a useful stock pot in which bones and other remnants could be reduced to form the basis of soups etc.

It was originally invented in France at the end of the 18th C., but was not introduced into this country until the 19th C. After some initial disasters, the pressure was reduced to three pounds, after which the weighted valve on the pot lid lifted to release the steam.

By the mid 19th C. it was in common use and is mentioned in Mrs. Beeton's cookery book.

Kettles (48) in the form which we know them today did not come into common use much before the end of the 17th C. Although made in various sizes, they have always retained their present basic shape, which makes them difficult to date.

Copper kettles (51) which heated water more quickly than those of cast iron, tended to have a shorter working life, and unless carefully looked after, were apt to require frequent repairs. Soldering of the joints and edges was done by intinerant tinkers.

With the increasing popularity of tea drinking, copper kettles were used in the parlours as well as in the kitchens of the wealthy, whereas the heavy cast iron black kettle was the main vehicle for providing hot water for the poorer classes. From the early 19th C. it was often equipped with the ingenious *Kettle Tilter* (48) which meant that one did not have to lift the heavy kettle from its hanger to pour out water, nor to dirty one's hands in so doing.

Even refilling could be done from a jug, so that in some cottages the kettle and tilter suspended from the small crane over the bar grate became something of a permanent fixture.

The only exception to the normal shape was the *Half Kettle* (51) which as its name implies was in fact made in the form of half a copper kettle cut through vertically with one flat side. This enabled it, when placed on a fire bar extension, to be put tight up against the fire, and so to provide hot water as speedily as possible.

Half kettles were usually quite small, with a capacity of about a pint, and used for hot drinks or for keeping gravy warm. They are said to have been especially popular with 18th C. university students.

In farms and large country households, where down hearths continued in use for much longer than in the towns, a hanging *Hot Water Cistern* (50) might take the place of the kettle. It held four or more gallons of water, and kept suspended over the fire, and refilled periodically, provided an almost permanent supply of hot water from its long brass spout and tap.

The greater width of the downhearth fireplace enabled the cistern to be pushed over to one side when other activities demanded the full use of the fire below. They were made in both copper and cast iron.

The earliest form of what we now know as a *Saucepan* was the 13th C. three-legged bell-shaped posnet or pipkin, which was superseded by the straight sided and shorter legged *Skillet* (52, 53) made in bell metal in the 17th and 18th centuries.

In Cromwellian times, the handles carried mottoes such as 'The Wages of Sin are Death' and 'Pity the Poor' but later these were replaced by the maker's name.

Although common at the time, many were later melted down for the value of their metal. In the West Country one of the best known makers was a firm of bell founders from Hatherleigh in Devon, known as Wasborough. Judging from the number of their skillets which have survived, they must have had a large output, distributed over an extensive area, including North America.

Saucepans (53) as we now know them did not come into general use until the end of the 18th C. They were made in a multitude of sizes, occasionally in brass, and more often in copper with a tin lining.

In larger houses pans would be adapted for specific purposes such as preserving and jam-making.

Double saucepans appear to have been used from the end of the 18th C., for a number of special purposes such as the glaze kettle (54).

Frying Pans (55) have enjoyed the same basic shape from Roman times, and probably before then. Those for use with downhearths were made of iron with long handles as the cooks who used them had of necessity to keep their distance from the fire.

The hanging types with overhead semi-circular shaped handles mostly of the 18th C. or later, could be suspended over the fire from pot hooks over downhearths, and from small cranes over bar grates.

Some have pouring spouts on one side, whilst others which appear to have been favoured in the North, have the spout under one side of the handle which is divided to facilitate this arrangement.

Finally there is the short handled type as used today. Early examples of the 18th C. were either round or oval shaped in copper with a tin lining and iron handles.

Towards the end of the 18th and early 19th centuries hot water *Steaming Pans* (57) were introduced with double linings both at the bottom and in the lid, as well as lift-out trays. They were used for cooking fish, hams, etc. The steam from the bottom part rose up through an inside flue, to condense in the double lid, and drain back to the bottom.

Mullers (58) in tin or copper were used for warming drinks of beer or wine. With downhearths the shoe type was used for pushing into the embers of the fire, whilst with bar grates the conical funnel type in copper known as an 'Asses Ear' was inserted behind the bars, the handle however was made in iron, and was much favoured in the West Country.

Recipes for mulled wine which varied from one place to another had clerical names such as 'Bishop' which was made from an orange stuck with cloves together with other spices, using red wine such as burgundy or port.

'Cardinal' was made with spices and white wines such as Hock.

'Pope' was similarly made with champagne, or heavy sweet wines such as Tokay. Mulled drinks require warming gently and should never be allowed to boil.

Gridirons (60) as their name implies took the form of an open iron grid on which steaks and chops could be grilled, or as it was then termed broiled.

The square types with short legs and a handle were used with downhearths, and the round types without handles for bar grates, supported on top of the bars.

Victorian examples had enamelled channel shaped bars connected to a larger transverse bottom channel, which had a small bowl at one end to collect the meat juices.

Another rather rare 18th C. item is the so called downhearth *Brander* (62) or as it was called in Wiltshire, a *Revolving Trivet*. Its use seems to have been limited to England. It was essentially a type of gridiron, rather than a trivet, in spite of its three legs.

A cast iron and enamel version with concave bars running back into a dripping bowl was produced later on in Victorian times.

Griddle Plates (59) known in the North and Scotland as girdles were essentially flat iron plates, either with a handle on one side, or with a hooped iron handle above so that they could be hung over the fire. The former required a brandreth in the case of the downhearth, or could be supported on the fire bars of a bar grate.

Circular tin rings were sometimes used so that Welsh cakes, and scones, could be made of a uniform size. Further information on griddles can be found under the section dealing with bread making.

The following is a relatively simple recipe for making griddle scones:
Ingredients:
1 lb. plain flour
6 ozs. fat — (1 lard and 5 margarine)
6 ozs. sugar
2 heaped teaspoons baking powder, (Borwicks)
1 egg
2 tablespoonsfuls of milk
1 pinch of salt
1 pinch bicarbonate of soda
¾ cup full of mixed fruit.

Making:
Rub the fat in the flour in a bowl, adding the baking powder, salt and bicarbonate of soda. Add sugar and fruit. Finally add the egg and milk to make dough, (not too wet or sticky). Flour a board and roll out about ¼ " thick and cut out with cup or pastry cutter.
Warm the griddle plate and grease top, put on open fire on a brandreth, unless you have a hanging type of griddle plate. Brown and turn.
The dough can be mixed in morning for use in afternoon, and the cakes will keep in a tin for a week or more.
But they are, however, best eaten hot with plenty of butter.
Salamanders (60) were commoner in larger households, and were rather like pokers with either a small spade shaped, or circular plate at one end.
They were pushed into the fire, and when they became red hot, were withdrawn and used as a portable grill for browning the top of bread crust, cheese toppings, or anything else which required heating from above.
The earlier types had long handles for use with downhearths, sometimes with two small feet added at the point of balance, enabling them to stand in a horizontal position. The end plates of the round type were about five inches in diameter.
It is claimed that early examples were sometimes used for touching off cannons, which must have been a distinctly hazardous procedure.
The later 18th C. types (77) were shorter and altogether smaller and without feet, and were pushed in between the bars of the coal fire to heat up.
They represent a good example of the change in shape and size which took place in kitchen implements due to the introduction of coal burning fires. Although now obsolete, some bakers used them up to the early part of this century, for browning the tops of oven baked buns.

44. A pair of cresset topped andirons *c.* 1730
supporting a plain 4' 6" long spit with an iron
pulley wheel. Above is a large and heavy cast
iron baking pot of five gallon capacity.

45. A black cast iron baking pot, with three
feet commonly known in the 18th C. as a
spider.

A 17th C. recipe for Bath Buns reads as follows:
'Mix together one-quartern of flour and a pound of butter, five eggs and a cup full of yeast and set
before the fire to rise. When effected, add quarter pound of sugar mauled fine in an earthern pottle and
an ounce of carraways mixed in. Add a little treacle.
'Make into little cakes the size of a pippen and place in an iron spider, and cover with cloth, to rise.
When effected put on the iron top: cover same with hot ashes and coals and surround the same, and
bake.
'These cakes are good with tea. If they are to be sent to a fine gentleman's table, omit the carraways:
split and butter and insert berries or fruit and pile same on top. Whisk some fresh cream and add some
sugar mauled fine in earthen pottle. Put some on top of cakes and send away.'
A *Pottle* (87) was a small earthenware pot holding half a gallon, used for preparation rather than for
cooking.

46. A black cast iron cooking pot, 10″ × 9″ with adjustable handle and spur for hanging a spoon.

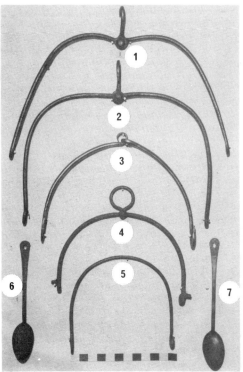

47. Pot handles. (1) Adjustable with top ring, and spur (see also 46); (2) As 1 above, but without spur; (3) Adjustable with linked arms (see also 45); (4) Individual type with top ring; (5) Ditto without ring; (6, 7) are stirring spoons, with holes in handles.

48. A black iron kettle fitted with a tilter to enable hot water to be poured out without lifting the kettle from over the fire; hung from a small double hooked bar the lower part of which is made to swivel.

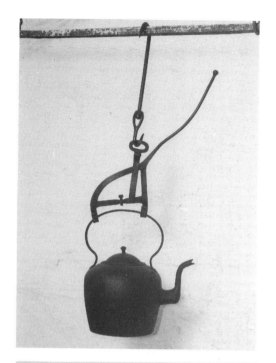

49. A 19th C. cast iron digester or early pressure cooker with iron hanging handle, the top being secured by lugs. The steam valve under the handle at the top lifts at a pressure of three lbs. As its name implies it was used as a stock pot.

50. Hot water cisterns, each with iron hanging handles and long brass spouts and taps. The earlier one on the left in copper, and the one on the right in cast iron. Each has a capacity of about three gallons, and when suspended over a down hearth and kept replenished provided a constant supply of hot water.

51. Two copper kettles, a copper jug which probably originally had a lid, and would have been used for hot water, and above a half kettle which when placed on a bar trivet against the fire of a bar grate would have provided hot water in a very short time.

52. An 18th C. bell metal skillet size four made by Wasborough of Hatherleigh, Devon. Size one is shown in illustration 53.

53. A bell metal, three legged skillet 18th C. bottom left. Two brass saucepans bottom row. Three copper saucepans with tin linings, top row.

54. A glaze kettle in the form of a copper double saucepan with worn tin finish and iron handle c. 1800. The circular adapter fits on to the top of the larger pan, and supports the smaller pan which is held in place by the raised brass band. The lid has a cut out section to take a brush. Glaze was refined stock in form of jelly which when melted was brushed on the top of pork pies, galantines etc. to improve their appearance.

55. (1) A long handled iron frying pan for a downhearth, early 18th C.; (2) A tin lined copper frying pan, late 18th C. or early 19th C.; (3) A similar oval shaped pan; (4) A similar serving dish; (5) An iron frying pan, Victorian.

56. Three hanging frying pans, all in iron. The left hand pan has the handle divided on one side to allow for the spout, and is Scottish. The middle pan has the spout on the middle of one side, and is English. The large pan on the right would probably have been used over a downhearth, it has no spout. 18th C.

57. Mid 19th C. fish or ham steaming kettle with inside container and lift out tray, 1' 4½" × 1' 0½" height 1' 0".
Incidentally the expression 'a pretty kettle of fish' has nothing to do with cooking. It is a corruption of the mediaeval word 'cottle' which was a kind of bag net or small trawl for catching migrating fish such as salmon or sea trout, and often used illegally.

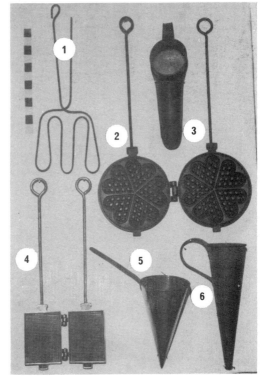

58. (1) A hand gridiron in wire; (2) A pair of waffle irons; (3) A shoe muller for downhearths, 18th C.; (4) A pair of wafer irons; (5) A brass muller with iron handle, for use with bar grate, typical West Country Asses Ear 18th C.; (6) A similar one in tin, 19th C.

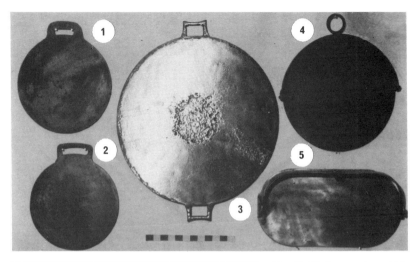

59. (1) 12″ diam. cast iron griddle plate with side handle; (2) 11″ diam. ditto; (3) Large circular iron plate 1′ 10″ diam. with two side handles, probably for use over a peat fire, for making flat oatcakes; (4) A black iron 1′ 3″ diam. plate from Brechfa in Wales with folding handle. This had its own brandreth; (5) A heavy oblong plate with folding handle 1′ 7″ × 10″. Richmond, York.

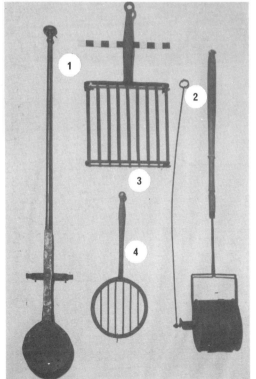

60. (1) A late 17th C. Salamander with feet at the point of balance; (2) A coffee bean roaster for a down hearth fire, the lid for the drum is at the bottom, and is revolved by the side arm; (3) Square gridiron with short feet for downhearths; (4) A round gridiron without feet for bar grates.

61. A hanging brander, a localised version of
a griddle from Inverness and Rosshire.

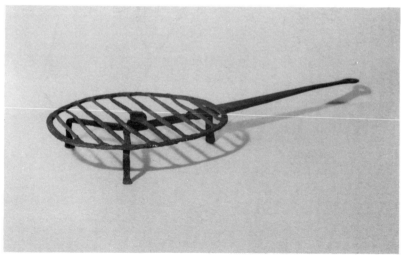

62. A revolving trivet, or so called down
hearth brander, a rare type of English gridiron.

Baking Bread etc.

In the North *Bread Ovens* were rarely built except in the larger houses and castles; but where they were used they were usually built adjacent to the cooking fire. They were constructed separately, being formed about two feet six inches above the floor level, and were usually between two or three feet in diameter, with a slightly domed roof about eighteen inches high in the middle.

Although an iron door and frame were commonly used (63) in some cases a two inch thick oak door reinforced with iron straps served the purpose, as presumably it had done before iron doors became generally available. Although it might become charred at the back, it no doubt lasted for a considerable time, especially if daubed with clay, which in some cases appears to have been used to keep the wooden door in position.

The oven was heated with kindling, composed of dry brushwood or furze, which when ignited, and replenished as necessary, raised the heat in the oven to the required temperature. When this was reached the ashes were raked out. In some instances arrangements were made for them to fall through a chute into the space below, from which they could be shovelled out later on. The thrifty cottager did not waste the ash which was kept for lye making or spread on the garden, or alternatively sprinkled over the pit of the outside earth closet.

Firewood was gathered on a continuous basis, with all members of the family contributing to its collection. 'Commoners rights' would generally include the gathering of brushwood for kindling. Although he might not cut down trees or branches, he was entitled to take all the dead wood he could obtain 'by hook or by crook.'

In larger households a *Dough Trough* (65) would be used for mixing the desired quantity of dough with a special wooden *Dough Paddle* (70). Friday was the usual baking day, just as Monday was washing day. Sufficient bread, pies and cakes would generally be baked to last for the whole week. Breadmaking had many old superstitions, one of which was to be careful to make a cross on the dough to let out the devil.

Oatcakes in particular had a large cross so that they could be conveniently broken into quarters, known as 'farls'.

The dough was inserted in the bread ovens and the loaves withdrawn on iron spades with wooden handles called *Peels* (70), whereas when the heat was lowered after withdrawing the loaves, wooden peels might be used for inserting cakes and pies. After using the oven the careful housewife would sweep it clean, and fill it up with brushwood, which would then be thoroughly dried by the time the oven had to be relit again.

A flourishing pottery industry existed from the 16th to the 19th centuries in North Devon, which included amongst its wares a type of bread oven, especially suited for building into the West Country cob walls. It was known as a *Cloam Oven* (69), cloam being a vernacular word for earthenware. The mixture used in the manufacture of these ovens was reinforced with Barnstaple grit and was made by several potteries around Fremington, which lies between Bideford and Barnstaple, from which ports together with other pottery, they were shipped across the channel to the coastal districts of South Wales, and from the mid 17th C. even across the Atlantic to Newfoundland, and later to the tobacco plantations in Virginia.

The ovens were made in a number of sizes, the commoner ones being a little larger than a straw beehive, having a separate earthenware door, known as a cloam stopper (63) with either a single or double grip handle. These doors could be fixed into position with wet clay in the same way as the wooden doors referred to above. A Roman numeral was usually scratched on the top of the oven, denoting the capacity in 'pecks' of flour (71). Sizes varied from two to twelve pecks. They appear to have been the first prefabricated item to have been incorporated into domestic buildings in this country.

Later examples had the maker's name stamped on them. The method of operation was similar to that of the more conventional types. They must have been popular as they continued to be made until the First World War, and when not used for bread making, served for other forms of cooking. Whilst it seems probable that these ovens must have been used in other West Country districts as well as in Devon, the only Wiltshire examples known to the author were built into a row of cottages at Horton, near Bishops Cannings, but have now been removed when the cottages were modernised.

Where bread ovens did not exist, bread and cakes would be baked in the heavy cast iron *Baking Pot* (44 and 45) which was placed in the fire, using a low baking iron (19) as a stand, if not already equipped with their own feet. The hot ashes as has been previously explained were heaped all round and on top of the pot. In peat burning districts, and especially in North Yorkshire, a *Yetling* (66) was used. It consisted of a cast iron flat bottomed pan, rather like a griddle with turned up edges, and with an iron hanger bridging from one side to the other, having a ring handle at the top. A thick tin circular band fitted into the pan, being held in place by four small clamps. On top of this rested a domed cast iron lid, rather like a modern saucepan lid with its own handle. The peat turfs would then be banked round and over the top, whilst baking took place.

Another specialised type of bread making used the *Hanging Brander* (61) which was seldom found outside the counties of Inverness and Ross-shire. It was chiefly used for baking the large bannocks of barley or oatmeal which formed a staple part of the Highlanders' diet. It was in fact a form of girdle and could also be used for grilling fish etc. or for drying the splinters of resinous fir wood which served as candles.

An alternative and older method was to bake flat loaves on bakestones or griddles (59). They would then be browned off on bread stands which looked like small wooden easels in front of the fire. In Ireland iron *Harnens* (69) were used for the same purpose, a corruption of the word 'harden'.

In the 18th C. cottagers cultivated with breast ploughs their patch of ground, and grew wheat on a small scale. Their wives and daughters also gleaned the local cornfields after the last sheaves had been carted away. The grain would be taken to the local mill, and measured in the bent ash *Dry Measures* (71) which were commonly used at that time.

Later, however, as the rural population dwindled, and cheap imported wheat became available the small mills closed down, and individual patches of corn gave way to the cultivation of potatoes and green vegetables. It became easier for the local baker to provide the bread, and *Bread Scales* (72) came into use, as by law all loaves had then to be weighed.

Bakers would also bake other people's home-made pies and cakes, as well as those which they had made themselves; a custom used not only in villages, but also in towns, where even joints of meat were taken to be cooked and then hurriedly carried home under the large dish covers then in regular use.

Haverbread in thin flat loaves was made in the North Country until quite recently. It is said to have been introduced by the Vikings, and troops from the north of England carried it with them, from which originated the word haversack.

Large thin oatcakes were also made in districts where oats were the main cereal crop. The oatmeal batter was stirred with a wooden *Thible* (73) and cooked on a griddle, girdle, or bakestone. The oatcakes were stored on racks hanging from the ceilings, presumably to keep them from the mice, and were later broken up by means of *Ridge Rollers* (73), a special type of ridged wooden rolling pin. They were eaten with buttermilk, and would seem to have been the forerunner of our present breakfast cereal. Nowadays when bread can be bought in so many varieties, including sliced and wrapped loaves, it is difficult to appreciate how much the ordinary person in the 18th and 19th C. relied on it. Even in the early 19th C. a workman would consume about two pounds of bread daily, which would be eaten at every meal together with whatever else was available.

Nursery Rhyme.

Pat-a-cake, Pat-a-cake, Baker's man,
Bake me a cake as soon as you can;
Prick it, and nick it, and mark it with B,
And put it in the oven for baby and me.

Note. There is a large number of slightly different versions.

63. Bread oven Doors. (1) A double handled cloam stopper 1′ 2″ × 10″; (2) A cast iron door and frame. Chitterne, Wilts. 1′ 3″ × 10″; (3) A rare 2″ oak door with iron straps 20″ × 15″; Honington, Nr. Shipston-on-Stour; (4) A cast iron door 1′ 5″ × 1′ 2″ Royal Crescent, Bath.

64. Cast iron door to side oven with small door to fire under. *c.* 1790. Dale and Co., Argyle Street, Bath.

65. Elm Dough trough on 4 legs, with side flour compartment, Lid (hinges missing) and two side handles. 3′ 8″ × 1′ 9″ × 2′ 9″ high, trough 13″ deep. Herefordshire.

66. A yetling — a built up sectional container for baking bread on a peat fire. Courtesy of the Castle Museum, York.

67. An iron harnen or bread stand for browning the bread crust.

68. (1) A bent wood flour barrel; (2) An early hand cut scoop which could have been used for flour; (3) A horse hair sieve in a bent ash frame.

69.   A cloam oven for building into cob walls.
Courtesy of Tiverton Museum.

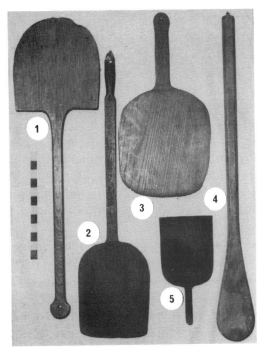

70. (1) Oak oven peel with long handle; (2) Iron bread peel (wooden handle removed) Suffolk; (3) Oak peel with short handle for taking oatcakes off a griddle or bakestone; (4) Dough mixing paddle for use with dough trough (63); (5) Iron peel head.

71. Standard but now obsolete dry or corn measures of bent ash. (1) Peck; (2) Bushel; (3) Gallon; (4) Quart. Note: 4 quarts = 1 gallon; 2 gallons = 1 peck; 4 pecks = 1 bushel.

(continued on page 65)

The dry measures shown on plate 71 were not only used by officials of weight and measures, market traders and shop keepers, but also by the housewife and her domestics. These measures when filled level with the top yielded a recognised weight i.e.

1 Peck	= 14 lbs flour
1 Gallon	= 7 lbs flour
1 Quartern	= 3½ lbs
1 Half Quartern or 1 Quart	= 1 lb 12 ozs.
1 Pint	= 14 ozs of flour

(see also appendix)

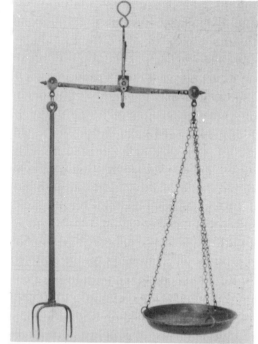

72. Bakers Bread Scales. The loaf was secured between the two arms on the left of the photo.

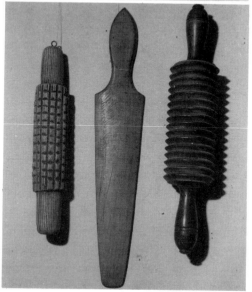

73. Two ridge rollers, that on the left is Welsh, and that on the right Scottish, used for breaking up thin oatcakes. The centre item is a thible used for mixing the oatmeal, and spreading it on the griddle plate.

Implements and Accessories

The great variety and number of items which might be illustrated in this category has made it difficult to decide what to include. It seemed better to put items of similar size together, even if in some cases, the ideal grouping had to be sacrificed.

As most of those illustrated, dealing with the preparation of food and drink are relatively small, it was decided to mount them on display boards, and to present them in this way, which enabled each object to be numbered, and a foot scale divided into inches included, so that sizes can be judged without undue difficulty.

An endeavour has also been made to group the items in such a way as to include those made of similar materials, and used for the same sort of purpose, whilst including most, if not all of the commonest items — as well as some which are not so common. It is hoped that sufficient have been included, to allow similar items to be readily identified.

During the period with which we have been dealing everyday utensils were made of the materials which were readily available, the commonest being wood, which could in many instances be shaped by its user with little more than a sharp knife.

The old plural of the word tree was Treen, and this has nowadays come to denote all smaller objects, other than furniture, which have been made of wood. Many items were made of two materials, usually wood and iron, for instance the cooper provided all sorts of iron bound barrels, tubs and vats, not only for daily use, but for storage of all descriptions.

Barrels were used for the purposes for which we now employ packing cases; in the 18th C., china and even clothes which were to be exported by sea to the colonies, were almost invariably packed in barrels.

As for ironwork, the local blacksmith, in between shoeing horses would make all sorts of domestic tools, as well as many more for agricultural use.

Horn was used particularly in Scotland, being softened by boiling, and in the case of spoons were shaped in stone moulds.

These simple tools, however made, all display one common characteristic, namely that of a natural basic fitness for the purpose for which they were required.

The illustrations and captions will it is hoped speak for themselves.

By the 19th C. factory-made items, especially of tin, were becoming used in all but out of the way places, as for instance the Tongue Press, the Steamer which fitted over a saucepan, and the spice box (88) as well as the complex steaming pot (57).

All these were the forerunners of the multitudinous, complex and ingenious kitchen accessories which were to flood the Victorian market, and which do not fall within the scope of this booklet.

It will be noted that the heart emblem was a favourite form of decoration on household utensils (41) and (82).

74. If the fire had been allowed to die down overnight and could not be resuscitated by the bellows, the old Iron Age expedient of flint and steel had to be resorted to; this entailed the use of the Tinder Box. The common form was a round tin box, often with a candle holder fitted to the lid. Inside was kept the tinder, usually a piece of charred linen, with the flint and steel, and a round damper for dousing the tinder after a light had been obtained.

The sparks from striking the steel (which was made in a great variety of forms) on the flint, caused the tinder to smoulder; a wooden spill dipped in a sulphur compound called 'spunk' was quickly applied, which caused a flame from which the candle could be lit.

The word 'spunk' which is gradually dying out of our present day language, is now used in the sense that if someone has not much spunk they are inclined to be spineless or weak-willed, and it is from the use of the tinder box that the expression is derived.

Right:

75. Metal Implements.

 (1) Toasting Forks (three) One home made out of thin twisted iron wire. One iron with intertwined hearts. Hearts were a favourite form of decoration on all domestic equipment. One cast iron from Lampeter.

 (2) Sugar Loaf Clippers 18th C. Rock hard Sugar loaves were cone shaped 18″ to 20″ high formed of hard white sugar. They were delivered wrapped in blue paper, and pieces chipped off as required.

 (3) Ember Tongs *c.* 1765. For obtaining a light by taking an ember from the fire, the projection on the front is for tamping down tobacco in a clay pipe.

 (4) Wood Fork. Made of iron with decorated handle, it has an upright tine to hold back the logs.

 (5) Apple Corer. A small example in tin.

 (6) Dough Scraper. For cleaning out dough troughs.

 (7) Nut Crackers. 18th C. Steel for use with hazel nuts.

 (8) Choppers. Small herb chopper for parsley etc.;

 (9) Meat cleaver with wooden handle;

(10) A late 19th C. potato cutter known locally as a Tettie cutter, a type peculiar to Devon;

(11) Wrought iron meat chopper;

(12) An all purpose kitchen chopper.

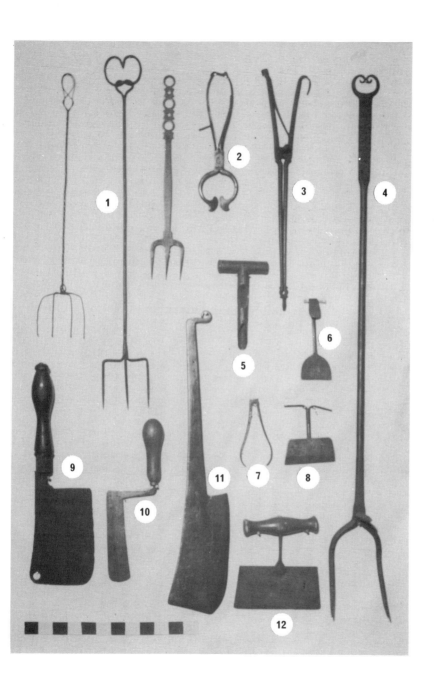

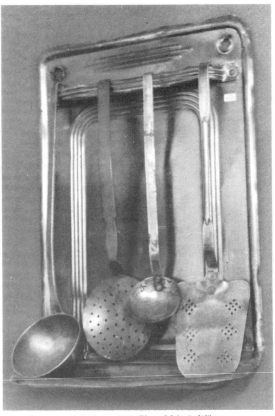

76. Tinware wall display c. 1810. Photo Melanie Wilmot.

Right:

77. Metal Implements.

(1) Meat Forks. The two right hand ones with three prongs 18th C. The single two pronged type 17th C.

(2) Wire Dumpling Scoop with Wooden Handle 19th C. Probably used in an institution where large scale cooking was carried out.

(3) Tin Spatula.

(4) Tin Ladle.

(5) Tin Skimmer.

(6) Small iron Salamander. For use with a bar grate 18th C. Compare with (60).

(7) Spurtle or Bread Spade. For turning bannocks or oat cakes etc. on a griddle plate.

(8) Early iron Spatula.

(9) Iron Spoon, with hole at top of handle.

(10) Two iron Ladles, with curled over tops to handles to facilitate hanging.

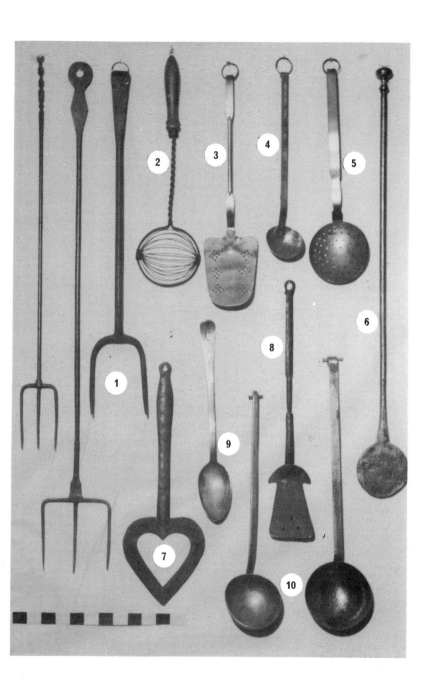

78. Wooden Implements.

(1) A Welsh 'paddle' Spoon for stirring the pot.

(2) A Lemon Squeezer.

(3) Two pastry Jiggers or markers, the wheels made of bone.

(4) A meat Tenderizer, similar to those used today, but in earlier days it is probable that their chief use was for pounding up hard dried fish.

(5) Two Potato Mashers. The basic shape remained the same for several hundred years. In the 19th C. potatoes particularly in Ireland were an important item of food. In 1843 before the Great Famine the average adult in Ireland is said to have consumed 10 lbs of potatoes each day.

(6) A large stirring Spoon.

(7) Said to be a Victorian linen Folder.

(8) A butter Scoop. With a carved mould on the handle for marking the butter pat.

(9) Two Scoops with hooked handles for hanging on the sides of buckets or bowls.

(10) A similar Spoon.

(11) A pair of heavy limewood Butter Hands.

(12) Six variously shaped wooden Spoons.

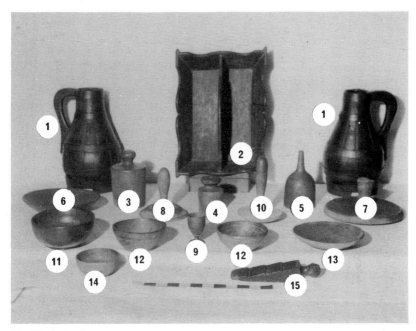

79. Wooden Implements.
(1) A pair of 12" high oak coopered belly shaped jugs. As is usual the wooden staves have shrunk when permitted to dry out. The insides have been pitched in an endeavour to keep them water tight. 18th C.
(2) An oak cutlery or Knife Box. With shaped side and centre handle *c.* 1830.
(3) A Pork Pie Mould or rammer.
(4) A similar smaller example.
(5) A turned kitchen funnel.
(6) A small cream Scoop.
(7) An 8" diameter sycamore Butter Worker to squeeze out the water. It could also have been used as a general press.
(8) A 5" diameter Cabbage Press.
(9) A turned oak Egg Cup.
(10) A Spinach Press.
(11) An early turned hardwood Bowl.
(12) A pair of small turned Bowls in sycamore.
(13) Similar to 6 above.
(14) A Salt Bowl.
(15) An 18th C. Mahogany Dish Slope. This was wedged under a big carving dish, so that the gravy could run to one end.

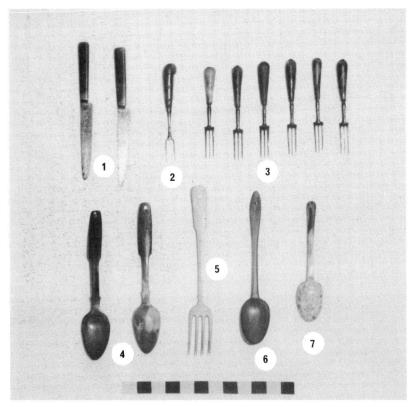

80. Horn and Bone Implements.
(1) A pair of kitchen Knives with bone handles late 18th C.
(2) A two pronged early 18th C. bone handled Fork.
(3) A set of three pronged late 18th C. bone handled Forks.
(4) A pair late 18th C. horn Spoons.
(5) A four pronged bone Fork.
(6) A single horn Spoon.
(7) An 18th C. horn Spoon with an engraving of a woman holding a bunch of flowers in an oval frame on the back of the bowl.

81. CIDER has always been an important factor in the West Country, besides being the popular local drink, it formed to some extent part of the agricultural wage; for instance in the early 18th C. the recognised daily free allowance in parts of Gloucestershire was no less than a gallon and a half for each day when harvesting.

This would be home produced cider made in the farmhouse, and used as the staple thirst quencher, as well as in some cooking recipes.

At harvest time large barrels would be taken in carts to the fields, the cider drawn off in jugs, which were used to fill up the mens' individual containers, such as the miniature coopered barrels known as a Costrel, which usually had their owners' initials burnt into the oak on one side, and scratched on one end.

An alternative container was the earthenware jar known as a Somerset Owl.

Both carried by leather throngs, would be kept near at hand by their owners whether cutting hay or corn.

For indoor consumption cider would be drunk from Mugs often up to a quart in size. Whilst the well-to-do used special Cider Glasses such as those illustrated engraved on one side with an apple tree, and on the other with a barrel labelled 'No excise'.

(1) Earthenware Cider Jug.
(2) Somerset Owl, mouthpiece damaged.
(3) Quart Cider Mug.
(4) Cider Glasses.
(5) Costrel.

82. Cottage spoon rack late 18th C. Note: Cut out heart decoration.

83. Whetstone. Domestic whetstone for sharpening knives. Late 18th or early 19th C.

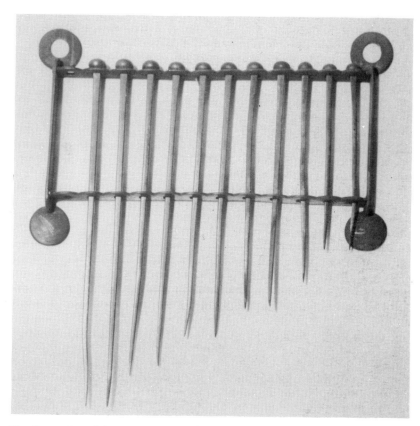

84.   Skewers. A set of eleven (one missing)
18th C. steel meat skewers in their original wall
frame.

85. A drop weight Mouse Trap
operated by an internal pedal which
on being touched releases the string
held trigger. A trap of this type is
illustrated in a picture of St. Joseph
dated 1425. These traps must have
been in common use for some three
or four hundred years; this example
is probably 19th C.

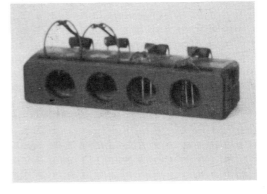

86. An oak home made four hole
Mouse Trap, the two holes on the
right have the springs held down by
the two cotton strands. The mouse
bit through the cotton to reach the
bait at the back. The spring
operated wire loop jerked its head
up, to be impaled by the projecting
nail at the top of the hole.

87.   Earthenware. (1) Glazed crock with spout and two handles; (2) White stoneware salting pot; (3) Part glazed preserving crock; (4) Dough mixing Poncheon, probably from Buckley Pottery, Cheshire; (5) Part glazed preserving jar; (6) Red earthenware pottle or mixing bowl; (7) Part glazed earthenware creamer *c.* 1840; (8) Ditto; (9) Ditto.

88.   (1) Tin Steamer with lid and side handles for fitting over a saucepan. Kendrick and Son *c.* 1850; (2) Salt Box. A 19th C. staved box with lid, alternatively light (laburnum) and dark (mahogany), salt boxes were usually hung near the fire, or stood in niches, to keep the salt dry; (3) 19th C. Screw down Tongue or Brawn Press; (4) 18th C. Brass Pestle and Mortar used to reduce pieces of sugar loaf, whole spices and medicinal ingredients to a fine powder; (5) A three tier Spice Box in sycamore, known as a Sussex spice box, each compartment screws into the one below. First half 19th C. (6) Tin Spice Box with six inside sections and centre one for a nut meg and grater 6″ diameter with brass drop handle. Probably S. Wales. Cost in 1850 2/-.

Index *Numbers refer to illustrations*

Bibliography

Antique Iron — Herbert, Peter and Nancy Schiffer.
The Blessing of Bread — Adrian Bailley.
The Book of Copper and Brass — Geoffrey Wills.
The British Kitchen — Doreen Yarwood.
Collecting Antique Metalwork — Evan Perry.
Collecting Bygones — Amoret and Christopher Scott.
A Country Life Camera 1844 – 1914 — Gordon Winter.
Domestic Utensils in Wood — Owen Evans-Thomas.
English Domestic Brass — Rupert Gentle and Rachel Field.
The English Home — Doreen Yarwood.
Food in England — Hartley.
The Home in Britain — James Ayres.
Kitchen Antiques — Mary Norwak.
Kitchenware — Jo Marshall.
Iron and Brass Implements of the English House — Seymour-Lindsay.
Life and Tradition on the Cotswolds — Edith Brill.
Life and Tradition in Rural Ireland — Timothy O'Neill.
Life and Tradition in Rural Wales — J. Geraint Jenkins.
Life and Traditions in the Yorkshire Dales — Hartley and Ingelby.
Treen — Edward H. Pinto.

Various Shire Albums, Museum Guides etc., and in particular
The Kitchen Catalogue of the Castle Museum, York. P.C.D. Briars.

Appendix

Hugh Roberts's interesting collection of antique cooking utensils, brings to life the items mentioned in late 17th and early 18th C. Probate Inventories.
A few members of the Wiltshire Folk Life Society have been transcribing such Inventories from the collection (held in the Wiltshire Records Office) of the Archdeaconry of Sarum. Relevant extracts give a picture of the housewife's (or cook's) equipment. In those days culinary success depended on skill in managing the fire.

INVENTORY taken on 25th September 1682 of the goods and chattles of
    Roger Marks, a Serge Weaver, of Little Cheverell, lists:

Item: 1 furnace, 1 bell mettle pot, 2 kettles, brass potts, 4 kittles, 2 skillets,
   1 warmingpan, 1 brass ladle and skimmer £4-08-00

Item: 1 firepan and tongs, 3 prs hangolls, 1 frying pan, 1 pr pot hooks,
   1 basting iron, 1 pr bellows, 3 irons candlesticks, 1 fleshhook,
   3 smoothing irons, 1 spit, 1 chopping knife, one fire grate 0-16-00

INVENTORY taken 20th May 1685 of the goods and chattles of William
    Harwood, yeoman, of Imber, lists:
   2 brass pots, 1 midle kettell, 2 small kettles, a skillet and skimmer .£2-10-00
   1 pair andiers, one spit, 2 pair of hangols, fire pan and tongs, a small
   pair of grates, a iron back, 2 pairs of pot hook, flesh hooks and frying
   pan, 3 iron candlesticks, toasting iron and trippet 0-16-00
   2 brasse pots pawned for 15s 0-15-00

INVENTORY taken 19th September 1692 of the goods and chattles of John
    Moxham, a Blacksmith, of Bradford-on-Avon:
   Two brass skillets, two bell metal pots, a little brass pot, a brass Pittle,
   one warmingpan, one sauce pan, one skillett, one basting ladle and
   one bell metal mortar and pestle £2- 0- 0
   One pair of Grates, one pair of Andirons, firepan and tongs,
   one dripping pan, 3 iron candlesticks, one frying pan, one pair of
   hangolls, two spits and some other items £1-15- 0

Note: We consider 'hangol(l)s' to be the local term for pothooks, trammels, ratchet hooks.

INVENTORY taken on 17th March 1722/23 of the goods and chattles of Philip
    Ballard, yeoman, of Bratton, lists:
   One Jack and four Spitts 10-0
   Five pair of tongs, four fire shovels and two pair andierons £1-0- 0
   A warming pan, four brass candlesticks, a Copper, a coffee pot, a spice
   mortar and a pessel and a pepper box 10-0
   Two sceeling boxes and clamps, three sceeling irons, four iron
   candlesticks, a chopping knife and clever 8-0
   One pair of bellows, a Candlebox and salt box .3-0

Three bell mettall potts, two brass potts, six brass kittles, three brass
skillets, three brass ladels, two skimmers, a little brass pott and a brass
fender £2-10-0
Four lattern pye pans, a cullender, a driping pan, six patty pans, a
sauce pan 2-6
One iron driping pan 1-0

Anne Ballard (widow of John Aldridge Ballard) let Bratton House to William
Long (already in occupation). An Indenture, dated 10th April 1746, after the
description of the house and outhouses, mentions 'an iron crane in the kitchen
chimney; a jack line and weights; a grate in the kitchen chimney for heating of
irons. . .''

E.N.F., P.C.H., J.M. and B.M.,
Members of Wiltshire Folk Life Society.

UNITS OF WEIGHT ESTABLISHED BY CUSTOM
(from a list exhibited in the Gloucester Folk Museum)

Bushel of Barley	47 lb	Bag of Cocoa or Sago	112 lb
Bushel of Oats	35 lb	Bag of Sugar	224 lb
Bushel of Wheat	60 lb	Barrel of Beef	200 lb
Sack of Flour	280 lb	Barrel of Butter	106 lb (small)
Chest of Tea	80-84 lb		256 lb (large)
Bag of Coffee	112-180 lb	Firkin of Butter	56 lb
(see also page 65)		Barrel of Raisons	112 lb

Elizabeth David in her book entitled English Bread and Yeast deals with such
posers as arise when using old cookery books — for example E Smith in the
Compleat Housewife (1746)
"To a quart of flour take a quarter of a pound of butter. . ." or E Moxon in
English House Wifery (1789)
"take one quartern of fine flour. . ."
On p.44 of this book the recipe for Bath Buns begins — "Mix together on
quartern of flour. . ."
In a recent recording of reminiscences given by an old man of 92, who was born
and brought up in Keevil, near Trowbridge, the writer was told — "His mother
made bread for the family. The dough was made at home. The cottage type
loaves of 4-6 lbs in weight were carried to the village baker in a laundry basket
to be baked. Potato was put in the dough to keep the bread moist (as baking for
his family occurred only once a week. They took about 7 loaves at a time to be
baked.''
The dough was probably made from 2 pecks of flour, the wheat having been
grown on the small holding, and ground at the local mill, with ¼ as much
(7 lb) added of cooked potato, together with about 14 pints of water. This would
yield about 52½ lbs of dough, which divided into 7 loaves would lose about 10
lbs in the oven, resulting in 40-42 lbs of bread.
Many of us still remember when we bought quartern and half-quartern loaves
from the baker — in the days before the Second World War, when they weighed
respectively 4 lbs and 2 lbs. P.C.H.